Do All Bugs Have Wings?

And Other Questions Kids Have About Bugs

by Suzanne Slade   illustrated by Cary Pillo

PICTURE WINDOW BOOKS
a capstone imprint

Special thanks to our advisers for their expertise:

Erin W. Hodgson, Ph.D., Extension Entomologist
Iowa State University, Ames, Iowa

Terry Flaherty, Ph.D., Professor of English
Minnesota State University, Mankato

Editor: Jill Kalz
Designer: Tracy Davies
Art Director: Nathan Gassman
Production Specialist: Jane Klenk
The illustrations in this book were created with ink mixed media.

Picture Window Books
151 Good Counsel Drive
P.O. Box 669
Mankato, MN 56002-0669
877-845-8392
www.picturewindowbooks.com

Printed in the United States of America in North Mankato, Minnesota.
092009
005618CGS10

 All books published by Picture Window Books are manufactured
with paper containing at least 10 percent post-consumer waste.

Library of Congress Cataloging-in-Publication Data
Slade, Suzanne.
Do all bugs have wings? : and other questions kids have about bugs /
by Suzanne Slade ; illustrated by Cary Pillo.
p. cm.
Includes index.
ISBN 978-1-4048-5761-2 (library binding)
ISBN 978-1-4048-6104-6 (paperback)
1. Insects—Miscellanea—Juvenile literature. 2. Spiders—Miscellanea—
Juvenile literature. 3. Centipedes—Miscellanea—Juvenile literature.
I. Pillo, Cary, ill. II. Title.
QL467.2.S582 2010
595.7—dc22   2009031834

Is there a difference between an insect and a bug?

Elena, age 8

Yes. All creeping, crawling creatures can be called bugs. Insects, however, are special bugs. Insects have three main body parts—the head, the thorax, and the abdomen. Insects also have six legs and two antennae. Butterflies, bees, flies, and ants are all insects. Spiders and centipedes are a lot *like* insects, but they have too many legs to *be* insects.

bugs

How many insects are on Earth today?

Christen, age 7

Too many to count! Scientists think there are about 10 quintillion (10,000,000,000,000,000,000) insects in the world. There are about 6.8 billion people on Earth. This means there are 1.5 billion insects for each person!

How many species of bugs are there?

Hannah, age 7

Which species of bugs has the most kinds?

Will, age 7

Scientists have named about 1 million insect species. They believe there are about 5 million more insect species yet to be found. Add 1 million non-insect species to that number, and your total would be 7 million bug species! Beetles easily have the most kinds. So far, about 370,000 kinds of beetles have been found.

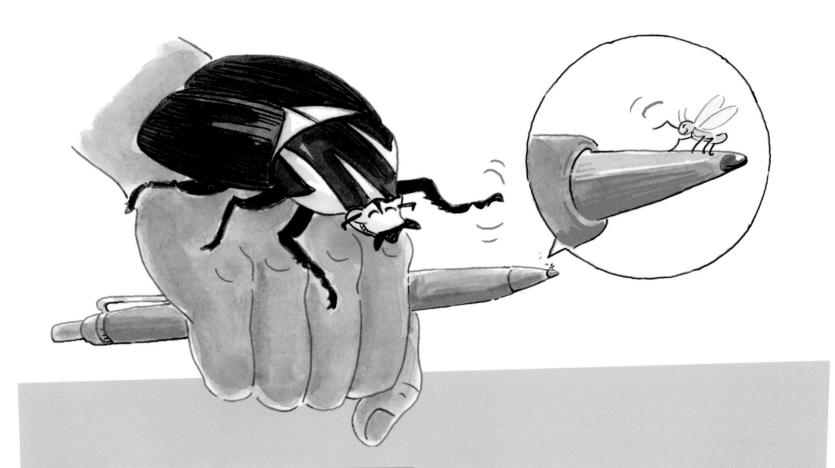

What is the biggest bug in the world?

Alex, age 8

What is the smallest insect ever?

Lathe, age 8

The Goliath beetle is the world's biggest bug. It can grow to the size of your fist and weigh up to 3.5 ounces (98 grams). The parasitic wasp is the world's smallest insect. Male parasitic wasps are 0.05 inches (0.13 centimeters) long. That's about the width of a pen tip.

What is the longest insect?

Dominic, age 7

A 22-inch (56-cm) walking stick found in Asia
is the world's longest insect. It looks like a twig.

Why do bugs have exoskeletons?

Conner, age 8

Exoskeletons have many purposes. They give bugs their body shape. They hold in moisture so bugs don't dry out. And they protect bugs from enemies.

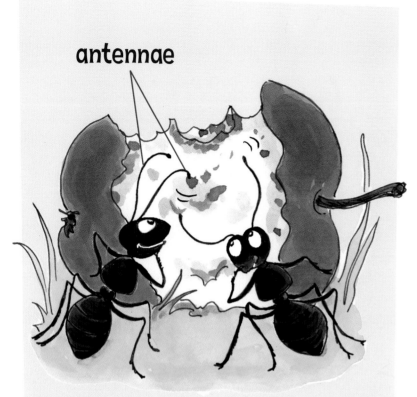

antennae

How do insects work their antennae so well?

Caylyn, age 9

Like your fingers, antennae are jointed. They bend easily. Insects move their antennae to feel, taste, and smell the world around them.

What are the body parts of an ant?

Kali, age 7

Like all insects, an ant has three main body parts: a head, a thorax, and an abdomen. These parts are covered with an exoskeleton. Ants also have antennae and powerful jaws. Some ants have wings.

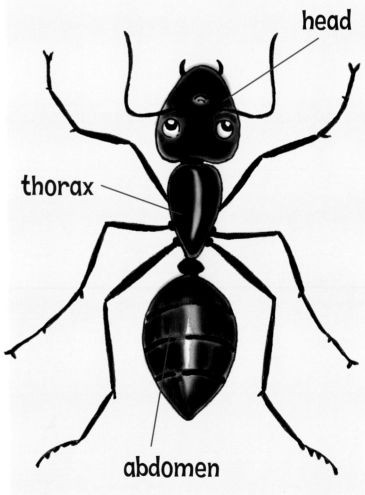

head

thorax

abdomen

Do bugs change color?

Sydney, age 9

Some bugs change color to hide from enemies. The crab spider, for example, is white when it sits on a white flower. But it turns yellow when it moves to a yellow flower.

Can bugs talk?

Sydney, age 9

Bugs can't talk like people. But they send messages in other ways. Bees do special dances to show where flowers are. Crickets rub their wings together to sing. Fireflies use flashing lights to send messages.

What do bugs eat besides leaves?

Izzy, age 8

Some bugs are very picky eaters. Others eat anything they can find. Spiders munch on all kinds of bugs that land in their webs. Groups of army ants eat small animals such as lizards and snakes. Dung beetles eat other animals' poop. Ticks and female mosquitoes drink blood.

Why do mosquitoes bite?

Billy, age 7

Mosquitoes don't really bite. They pierce, or poke, the skin and suck out blood. Only female mosquitoes drink blood. They need a blood meal to give them energy to make eggs. Male mosquitoes don't drink blood. They drink plant nectar.

Why do centipedes have lots of legs?

Brad, age 6

Centipedes use their many legs to run fast and catch meals, such as spiders. Even though their name means "100 legs," most centipedes have about 40 to 50 legs.

Why do bees make honey?

Alissa, age 6

Bees make honey for young bees to eat. It's like baby food. Bees also make honey for themselves. It comes in handy in winter, when pollen and nectar are hard to find. Bees must collect pollen and nectar from thousands of flowers to create honey. Luckily, bees make enough extra honey for people to eat, too.

Why don't cicadas come out every year?

Ryan, age 7

Some cicada species do come out every year. Other species, however, come out only every 13 or 17 years. That's how long it takes young cicadas living underground to become adults.

How do grasshoppers jump so high?

Karsten, age 7

Grasshoppers have extra-long back legs. These long legs have strong muscles to help grasshoppers jump high.

Why don't spiders get stuck in their own webs?

Timmy, age 7

Spiders use sticky and non-sticky threads when making webs. They walk on the non-sticky straight threads, not the sticky circular threads. Spiders also have special oil on their legs to keep from sticking.

What makes the color on butterflies?

Jason, age 8

Butterfly wings get their colors from very tiny, thin scales. The scales overlap, like shingles on a roof. They may be any color. The scales may also change color when light hits them.

Can you tell how old a ladybug is by its spots?

Carter, age 8

The number of black spots on a ladybug does not tell its age. In fact, some ladybugs have no spots at all.

How do ants build their homes?

Spencer, age 6

Ants live together in large groups called colonies. Worker ants do the building. These strong ants use their jaws to dig long tunnels underground. They also scoop out rooms. The rooms may be used as nurseries (baby rooms) or as places to store food. Worker ants dig more tunnels and rooms as the colony grows.

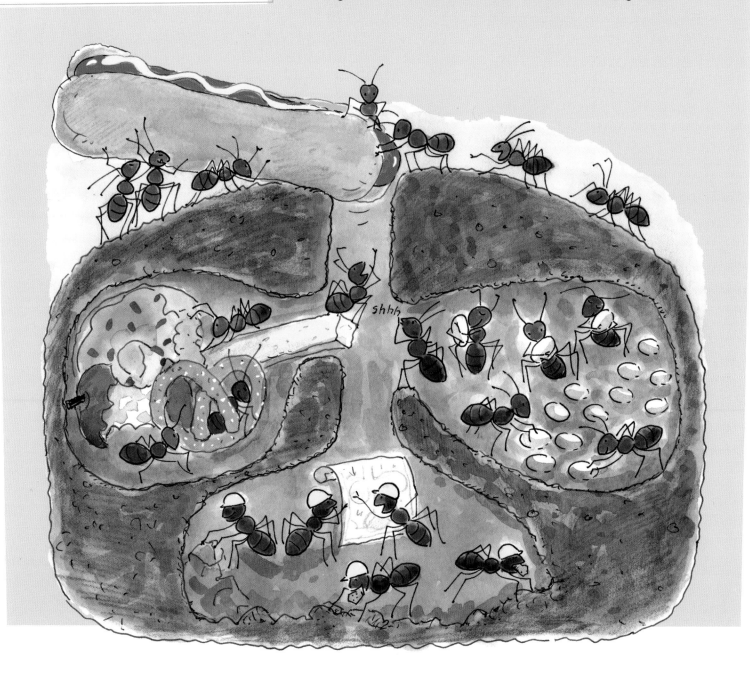

Do some bugs have poison?

Micah, age 7

Yes. Some bugs can make powerful venom. A black widow spider's venom is 15 times stronger than a rattlesnake's. Spiders deliver their venom through long sharp teeth called fangs. So do centipedes. Hornets, ants, bees, and wasps have stings filled with venom to protect themselves.

Do all bugs have wings?

Jenson, age 7

No, but most bugs do. Wings help bees fly to flowers to drink nectar. They help dragonflies chase down dinner. And they help butterflies travel, or migrate, to warmer places in winter.

Why do bees sting you?

Madison, age 7

Bees use their stings to protect and defend the colony. They often sting when a person or animal gets too close to their hive. Bees also sting if they are stepped on or grabbed.

What is the most dangerous bug?

Jax, age 7

Mosquitoes kill more people than all other bugs combined. Mosquitoes spread deadly illnesses such as malaria, yellow fever, and West Nile virus to more than 300 million people each year.

How do bugs make new bugs?
Kara, age 10

Where do bugs lay eggs?
Xayvion, age 8

Most bugs populate, or make new bugs, by laying eggs. The eggs of different bugs hatch and grow in different ways. Bugs look for safe places to lay eggs. Ladybugs hide their eggs under leaves. Bees lay eggs in a hive, inside small cells. Spiders wrap their eggs in a silk cocoon and hide the egg sac from enemies.

Complete Metamorphosis of a Beetle

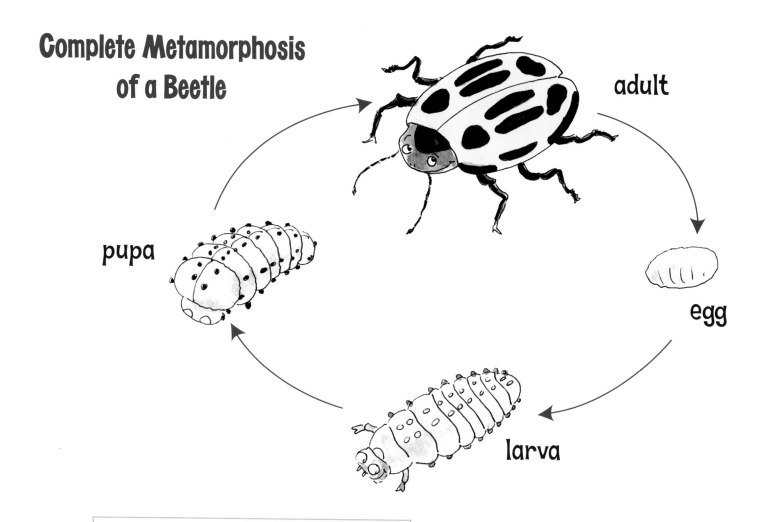

adult

egg

larva

pupa

How do insects grow?

Andy, age 8

Insects grow into adults in two ways—complete or incomplete metamorphosis. Insects that go through complete metamorphosis, such as beetles and butterflies, hatch from eggs as larvae. Larvae eat, grow, and turn into pupae. Pupae rest and undergo big changes before becoming adults. Other insects, such as grasshoppers, go through incomplete metamorphosis. Their young look like small adults. All insects shed their outer skin as they grow.

How long have bugs been alive?

Isaiah, age 8

Bugs have been around for about 400 million years. This date comes from ancient bugs that were trapped in tree sap. Over time, the sticky sap dried and changed into hard amber. Scientists can easily study these ancient bugs through the amber's clear yellow surface.

Dr. Ian Zekt

TO LEARN MORE

More Books to Read

Hudak, Heather C. *Insects.* New York: Weigl Publishers Inc., 2005.

O'Hare, Ted. *Insects.* Vero Beach, Fla.: Rourke Pub., 2006.

Pyers, Greg. *Why Am I an Insect?* Chicago: Raintree, 2006.

Richardson, Adele. *Insects.* Mankato, Minn.: Capstone Press, 2005.

Internet Sites

FactHound offers a safe, fun way to find Internet sites related to this book. All of the sites have been researched by our staff.

Here's all you do:

Visit *www.facthound.com*

FactHound will fetch the best sites for you!

GLOSSARY

abdomen—the last of an insect's three main parts, attached to the thorax

antenna—a feeler on a bug's head used to feel, taste, and smell; *antennae* means more than one antenna.

exoskeleton—a hard shell or covering that protects a bug's soft body

larva—the stage of a bug's growth between egg and pupa; *larvae* means more than one larva.

metamorphosis—the changing process from egg to adult

nectar—a sweet liquid found in flowers

pollen—a powder made by flowers

pupa—the stage of a bug's growth between larva and adult; *pupae* means more than one pupa.

species—groups of plants or animals that have many things in common

thorax—the middle part of an insect's three main parts, between the head and abdomen

venom—the poison of some snakes, spiders, and other animals

INDEX

Look for all of the titles in the Kids' Questions series:

Did Dinosaurs Eat People?
And Other Questions Kids Have About Dinosaurs

Do All Bugs Have Wings?
And Other Questions Kids Have About Bugs

How Do Tornadoes Form?
And Other Questions Kids Have About Weather

What Is the Moon Made Of?
And Other Questions Kids Have About Space

What's Inside a Rattlesnake's Rattle?
And Other Questions Kids Have About Snakes

Who Invented Basketball?
And Other Questions Kids Have About Sports

Why Do Dogs Drool?
And Other Questions Kids Have About Dogs

Why Do My Teeth Fall Out?
And Other Questions Kids Have About the Human Body